Little One
You're So Lucky

Dedicated to
Blanche and Bob Hardison.
I promise you will not be forgotten.
I love you forever.
~Mandy

Little one you're so lucky.
I hope you know it's true.
You have a special angel
who watches over you.

1.

2.

I know you don't remember,
But once upon a time
Lived a special person
Who had to say goodbye.

3.

Oh how they would have loved you, and enjoyed seeing you grow.

5.

Even though they aren't here anymore, theirs is a name that you should know.

Old photos

They meant a lot to me
and I miss them every day.

7.

It made me very sad
when they had to go away.

You make me so happy.
My heart melts when you smile.
Thanks for letting me talk
and remember them for a while.

9.

10.

All of the things I learned from them I am going to teach to you.

11.

Their memory will live on
in everything we do.

12.

13.

They taught me to be kind
and to always trust my heart.
They taught me that
they can still love me,
even though we are apart.

14.

I know they will look out for you
the way that Angels do.

15.

They protected me while they were here and now they are watching over you.

16.

Every night before you sleep
say a little prayer.
You may not see them
but I know they are there.

18.

CPSIA information can be obtained
at www.ICGtesting.com
Printed in the USA
LVHW071106200223
739424LV00004B/42